Copyright Information

Deez ltd.

Skikda Algeria 21000

deezusma@gmail.com

Copyright © Deez ltd. All rights reserved. No part of this book may be reproduced, stored in a retrieval system, or transmitted by any means without the written permission of the author.

DISNEY

ANNA & KRISTOFF FROM FROZEN 1

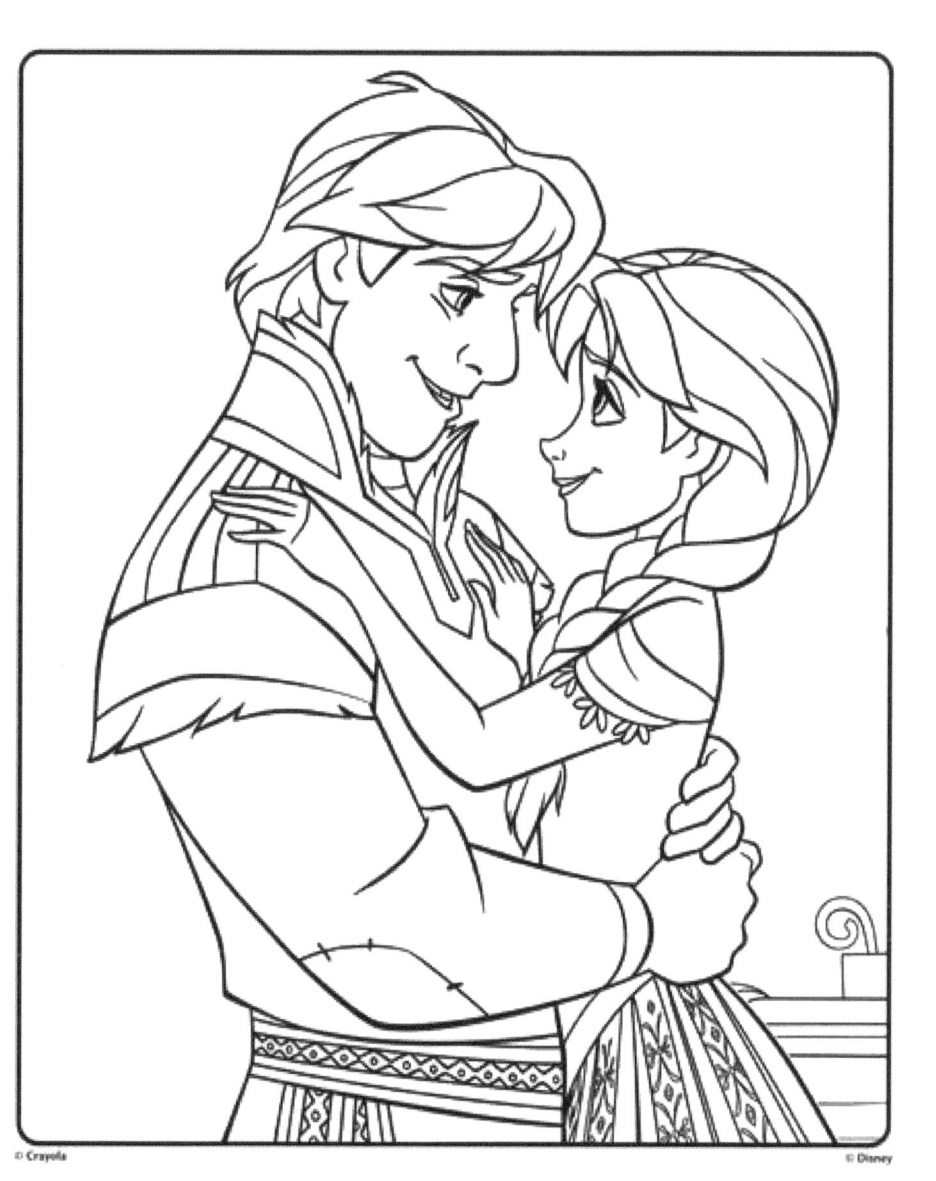

ANNA & ELSA FROM FROZEN 1

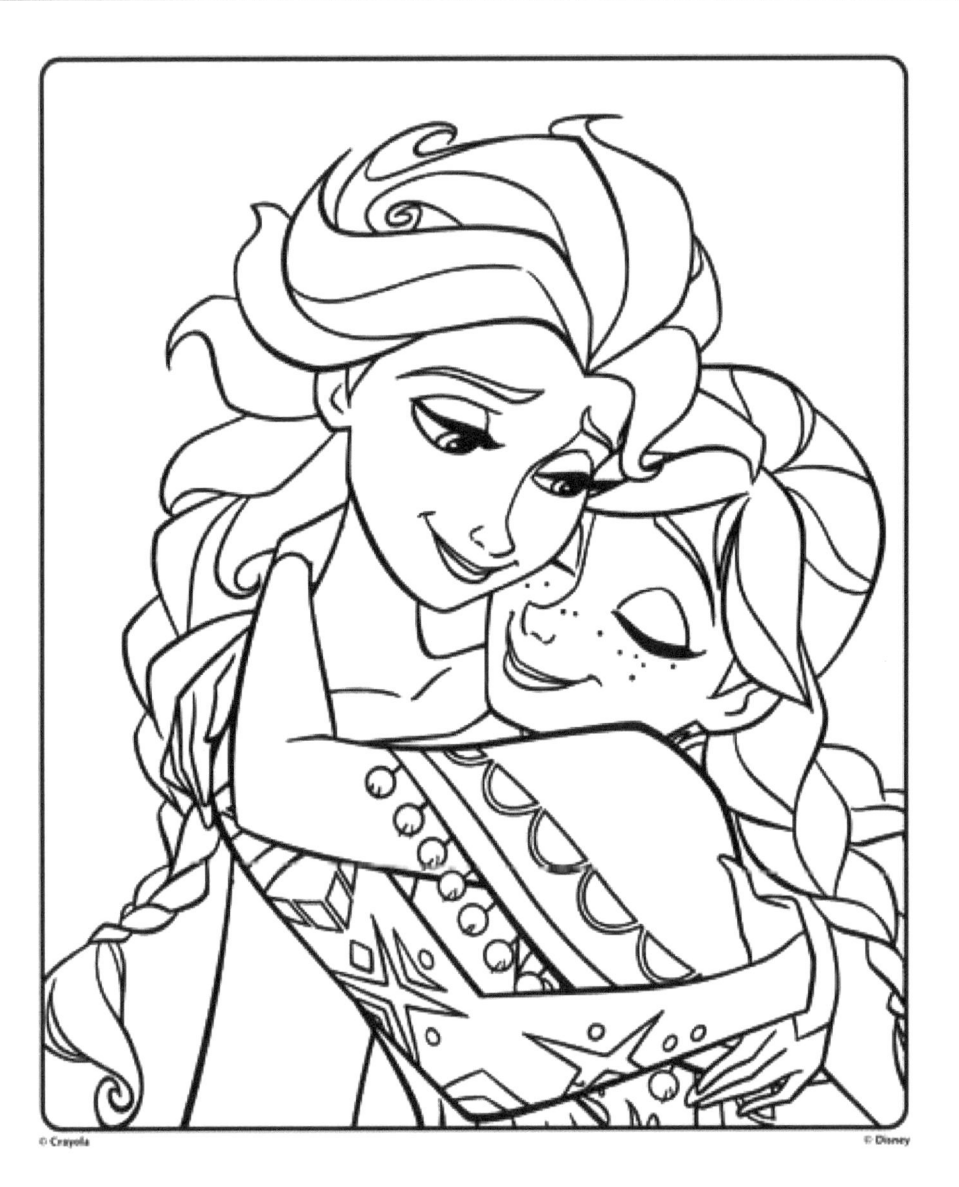

WOODY & BUZZ FROM TOY STORY

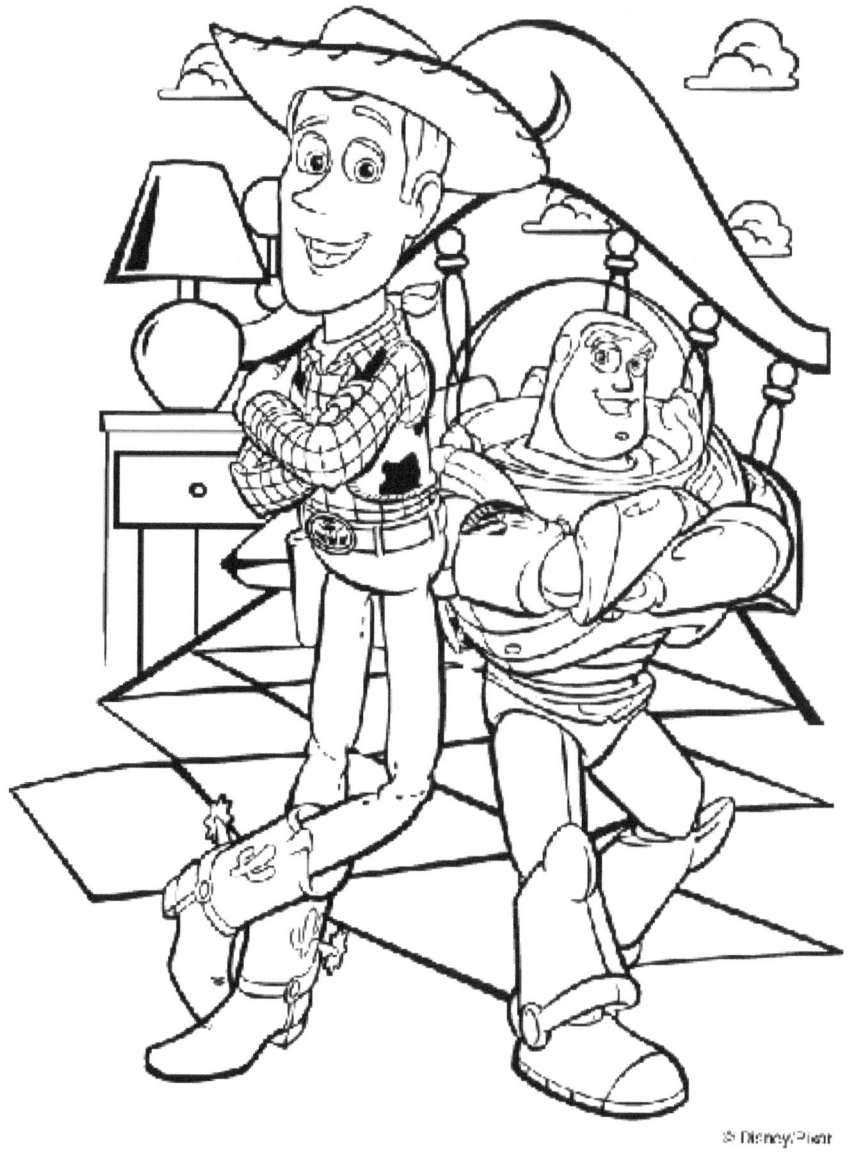

KRISTOFF CARRYING ICE FROM FROZEN 2

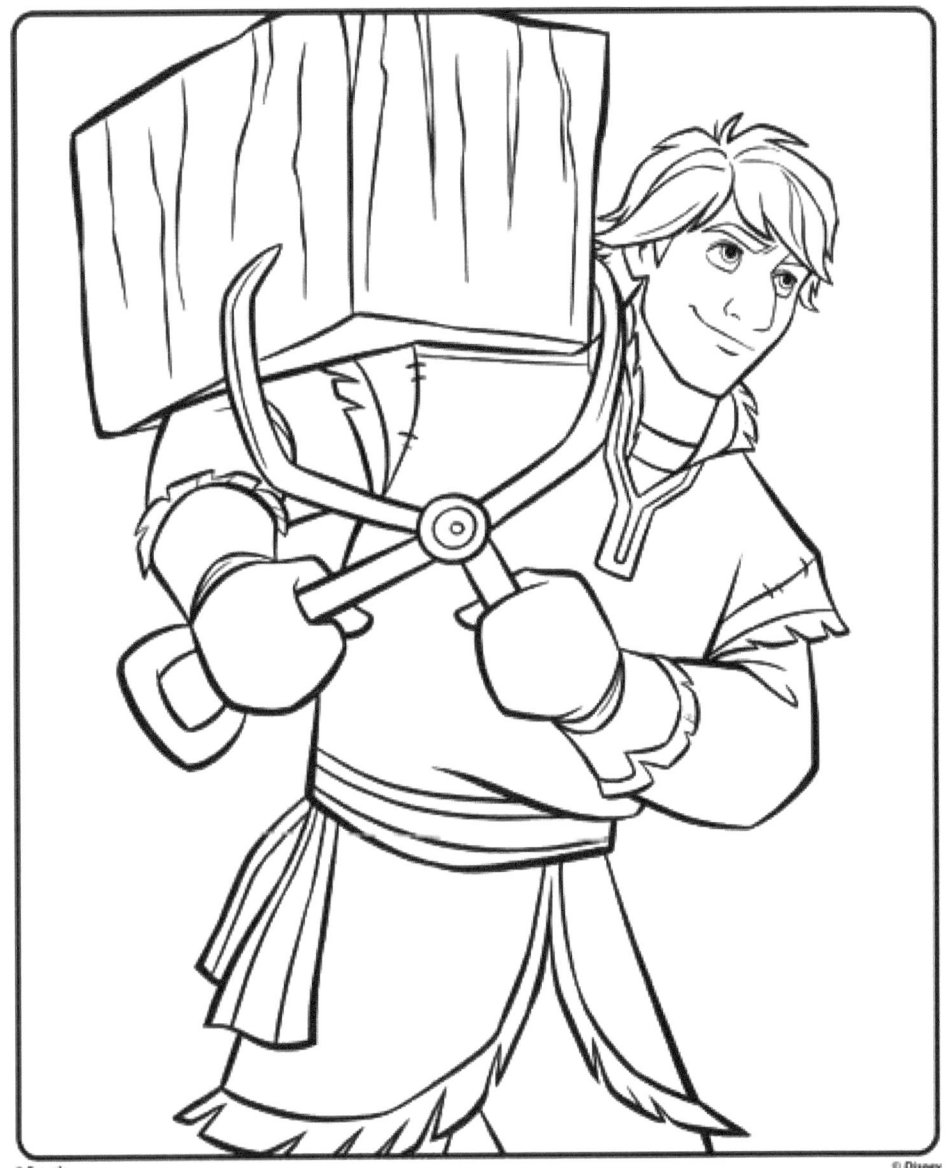

MICKEY MOUSE AND FRIENDS

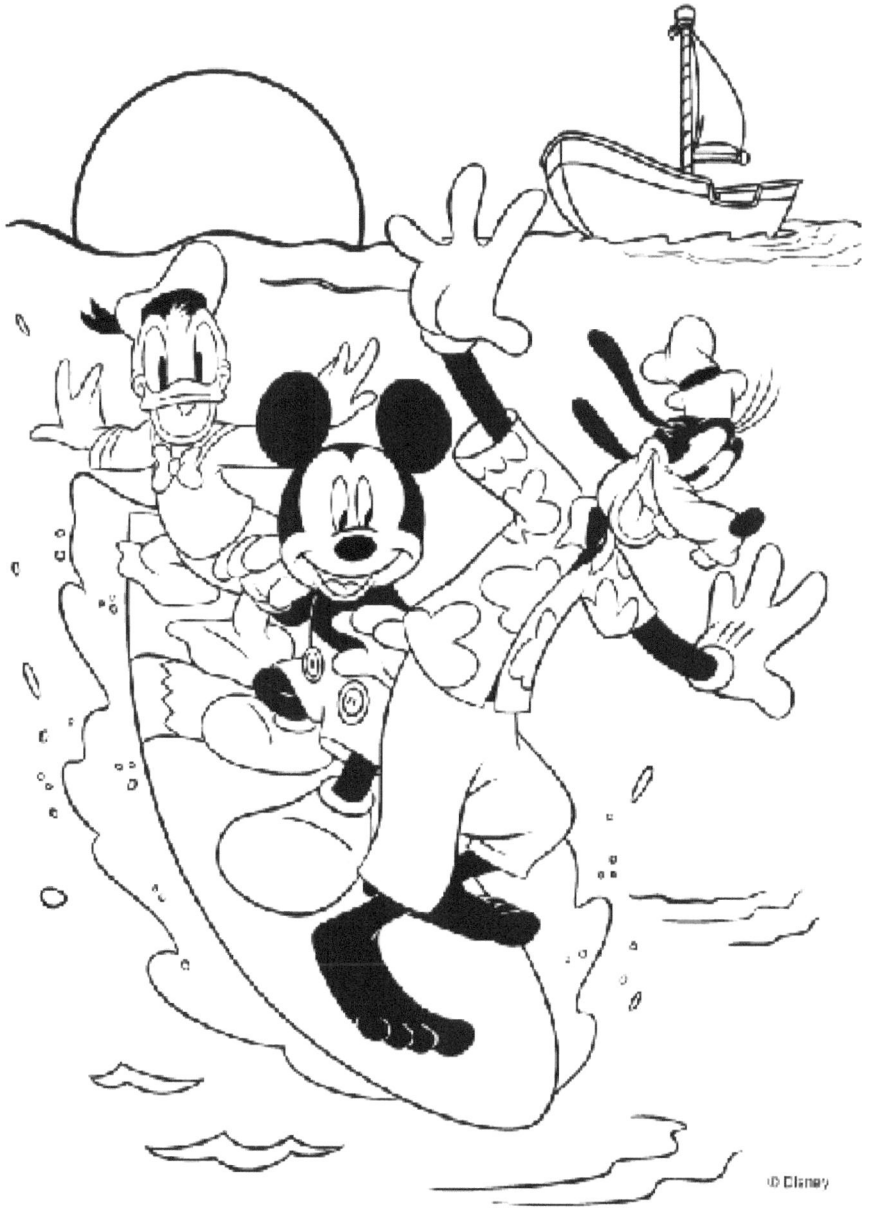

PLANTS & ANIMALS

SEAL

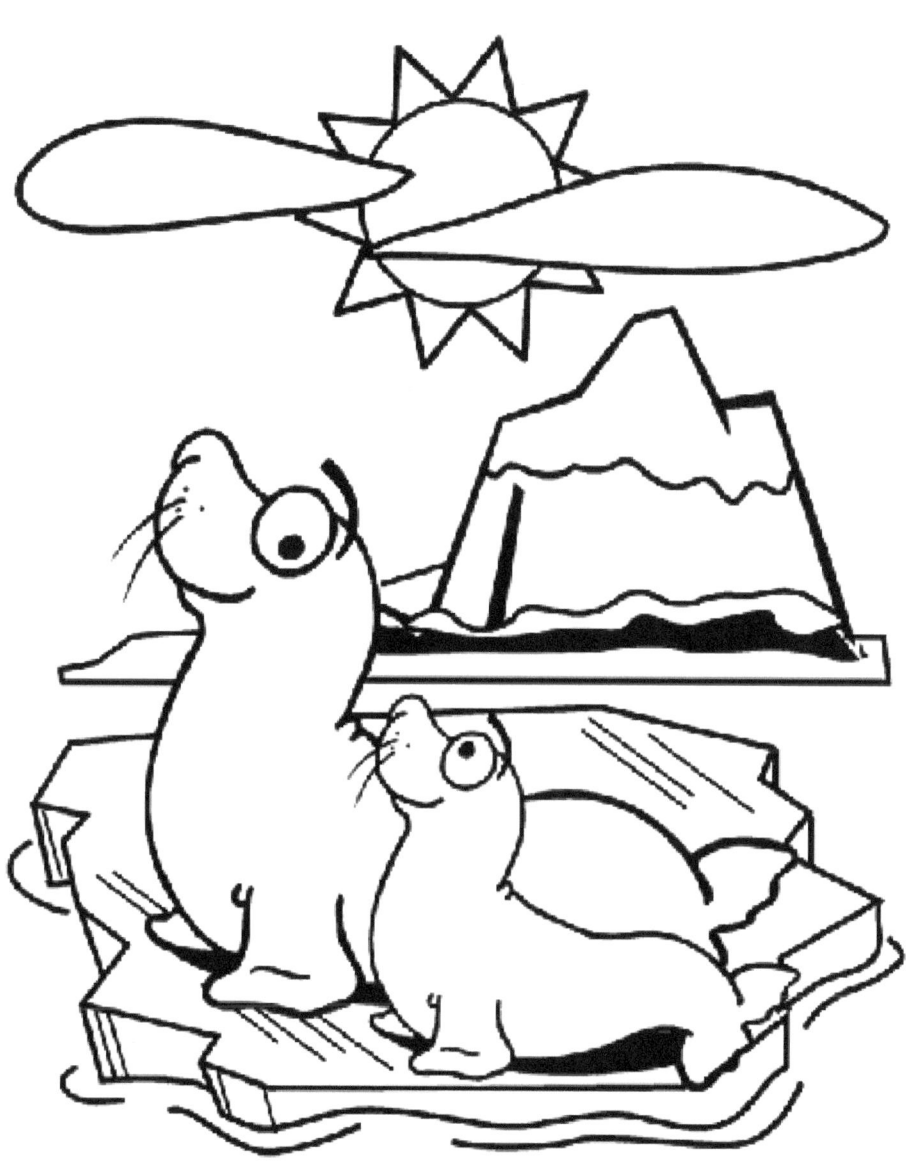

TURTLE MOMMY

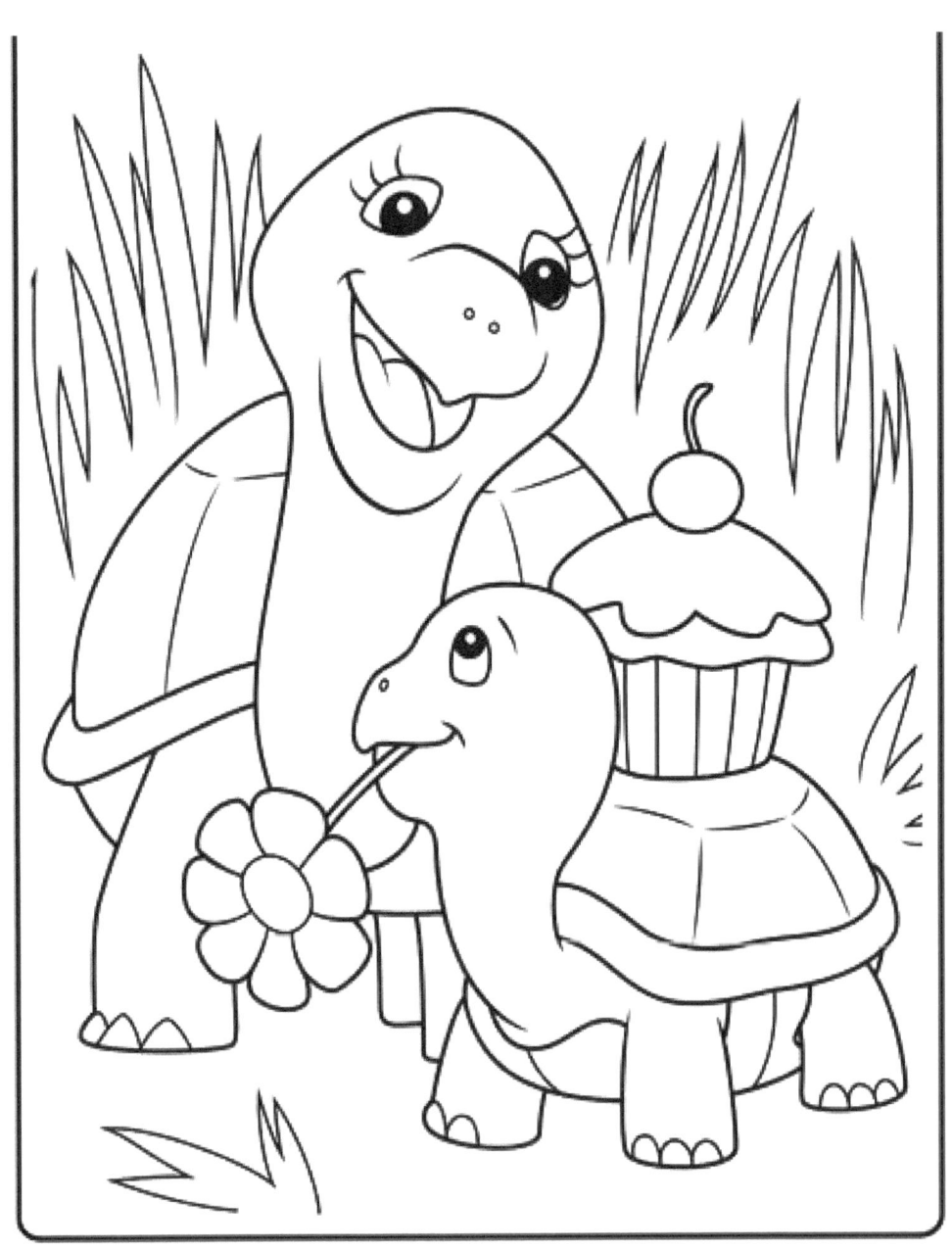

UNI-KITTY

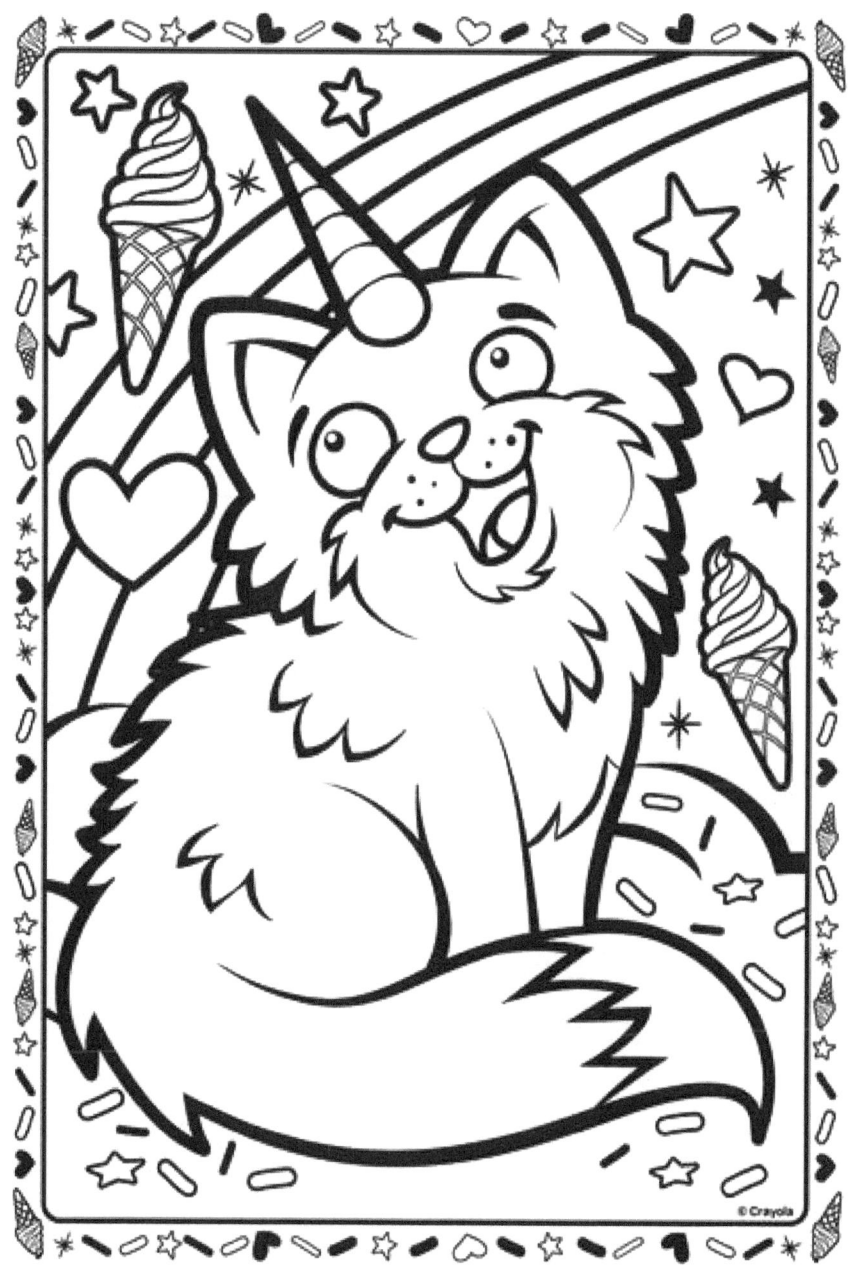

UNICORN IN SPACE

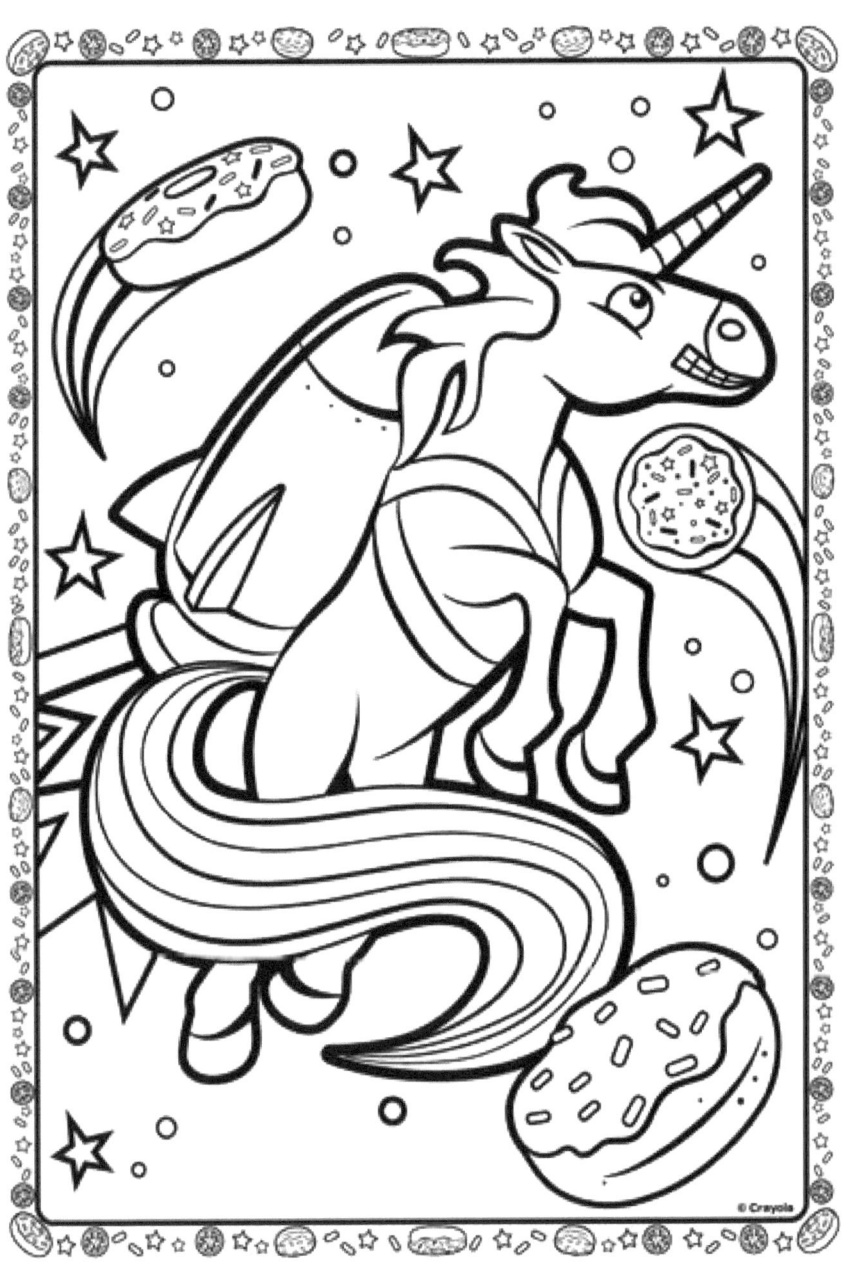

EARTH DAY TREE

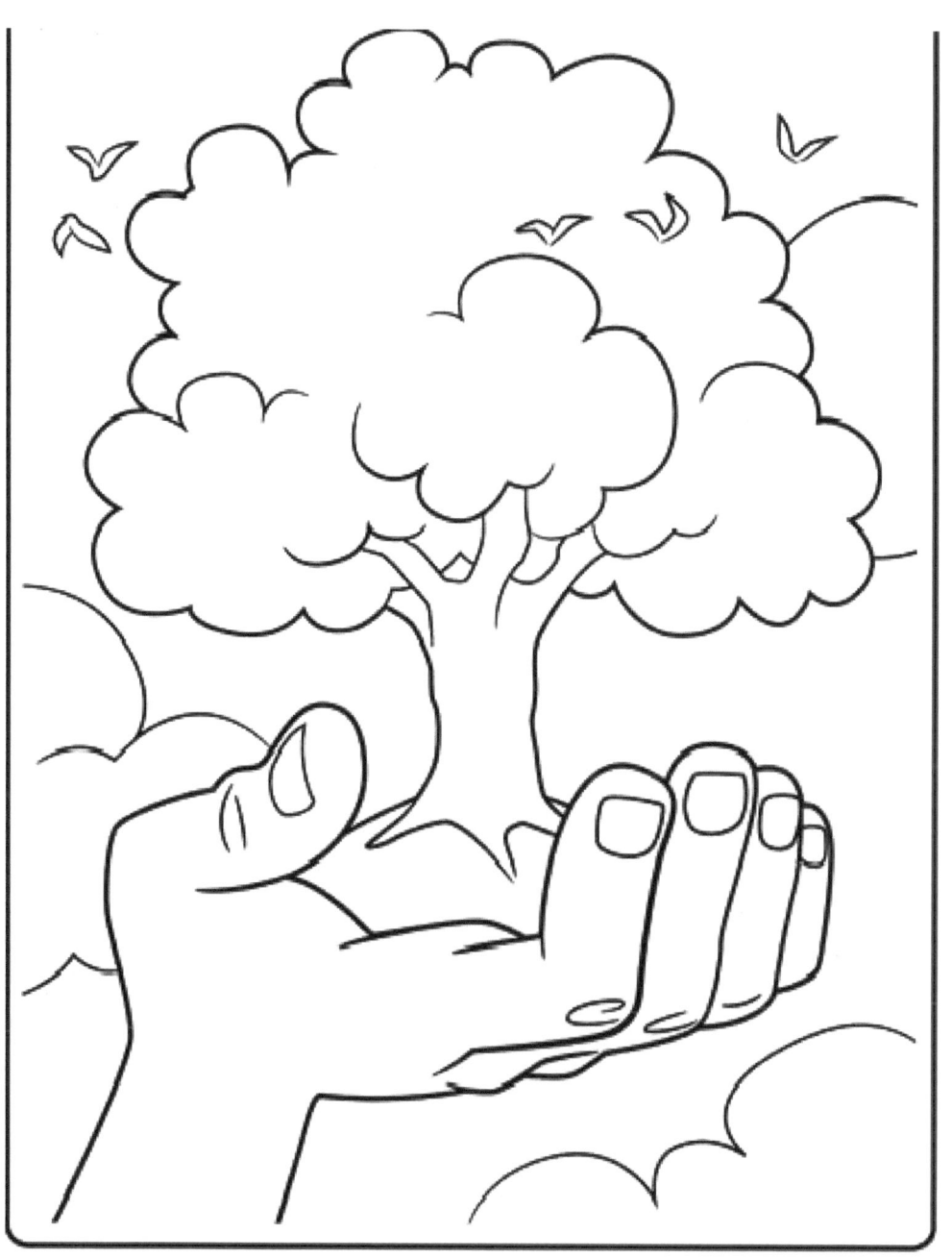

GARDEN CRITTERS

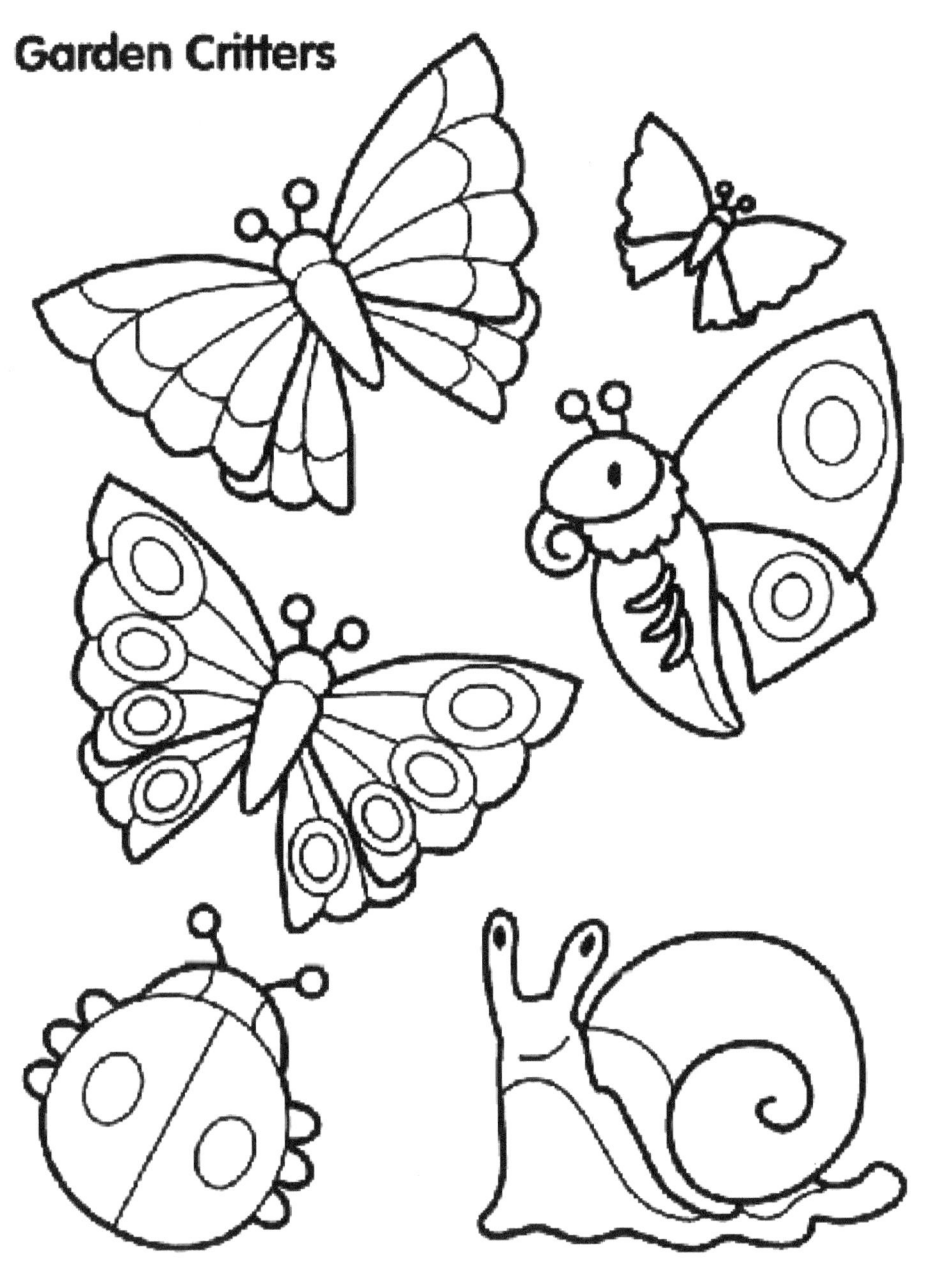

CARTOON CHARACTERS

STORMY

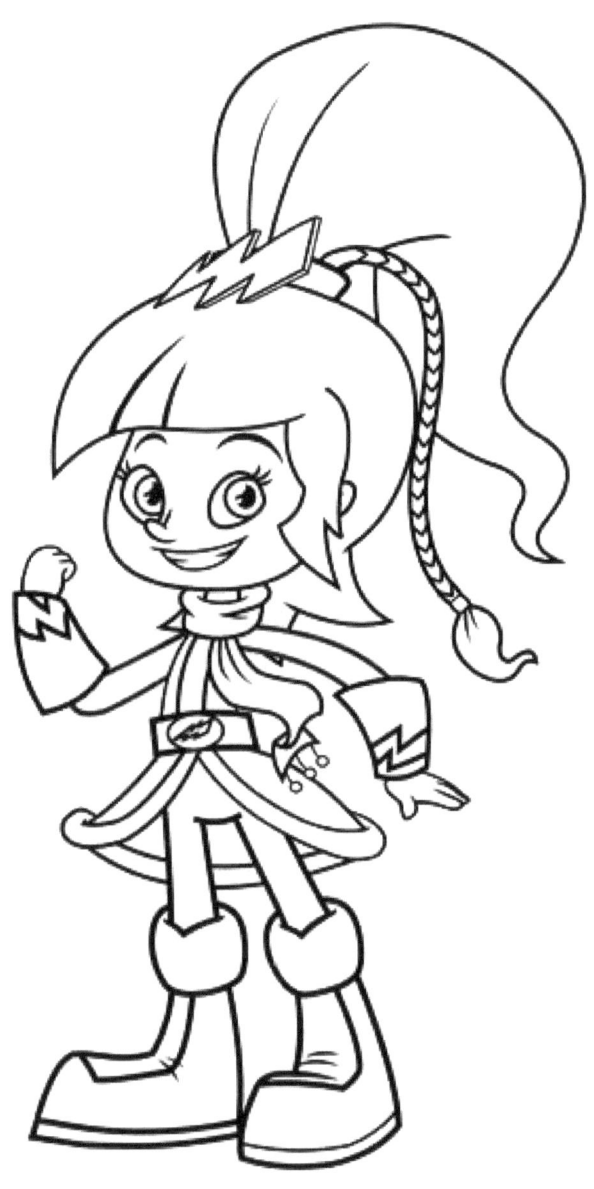

STARLIGHT

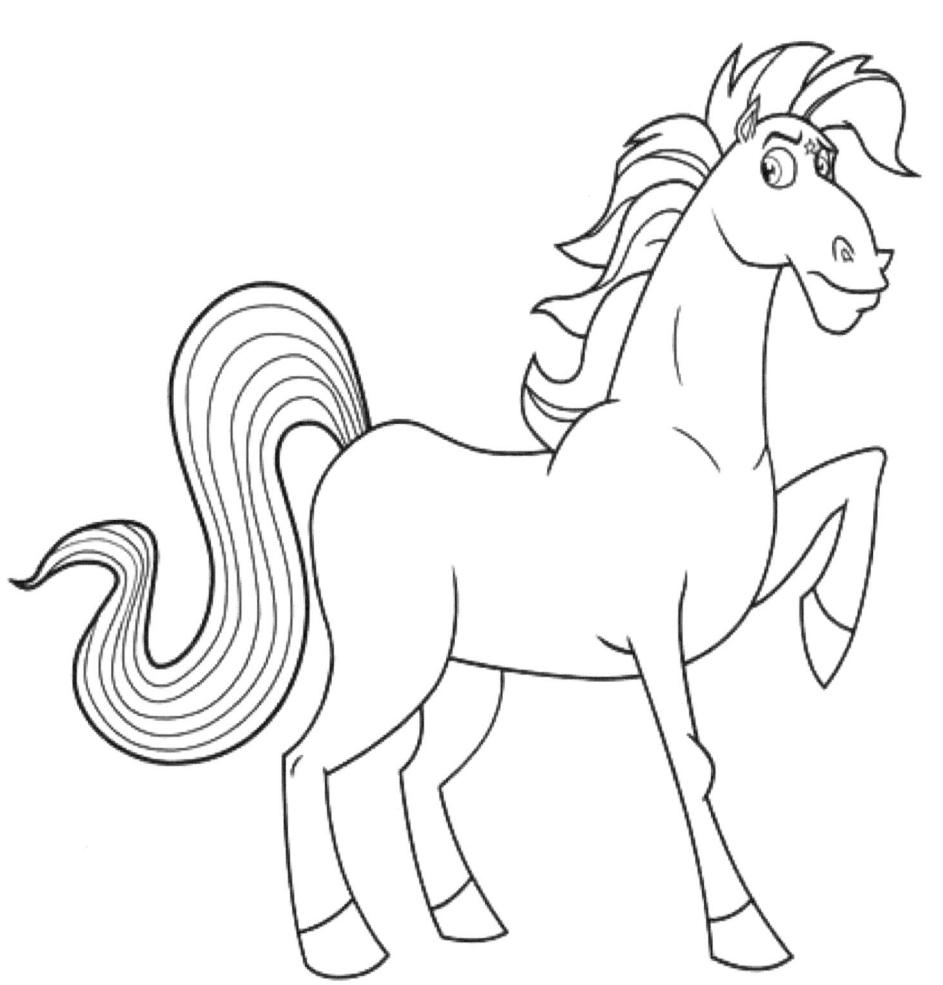

SPONGEBOB

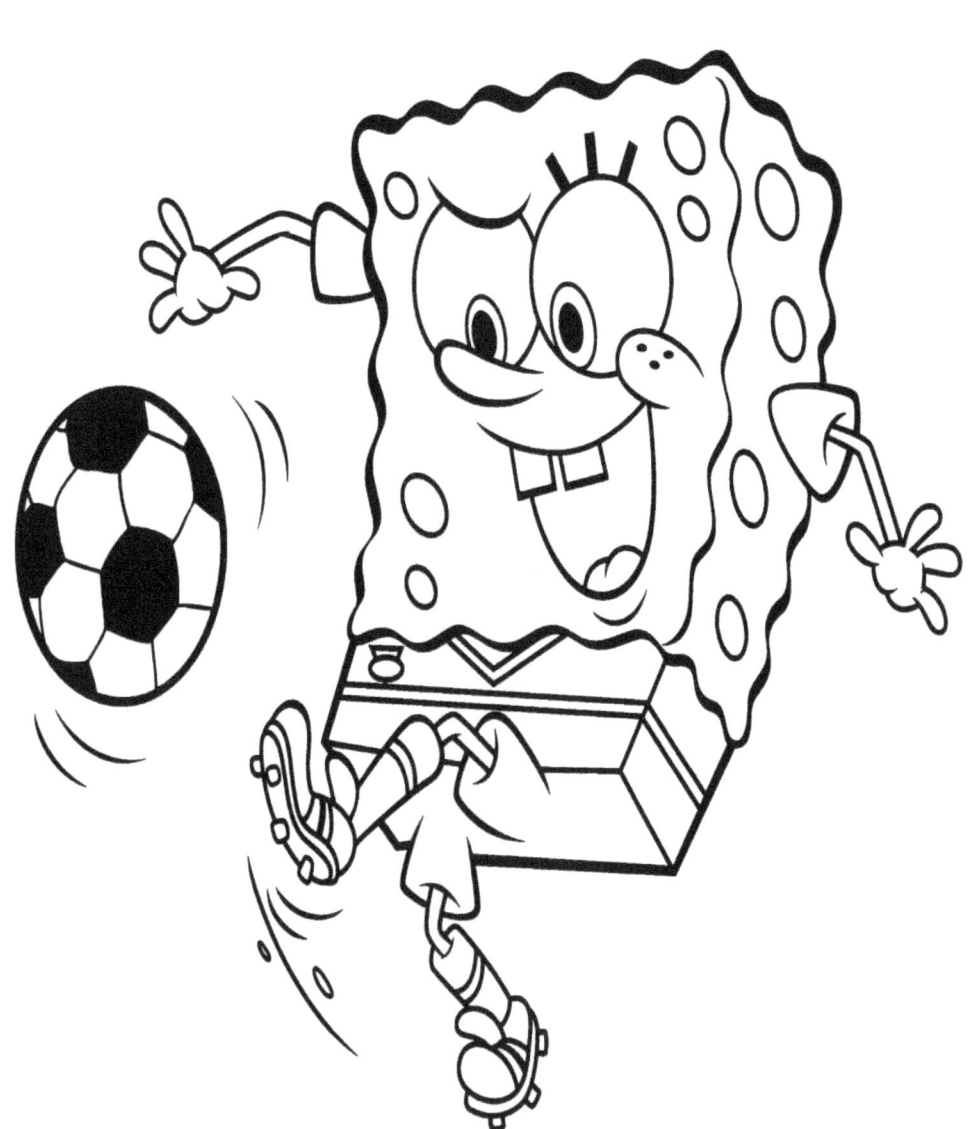

GARY

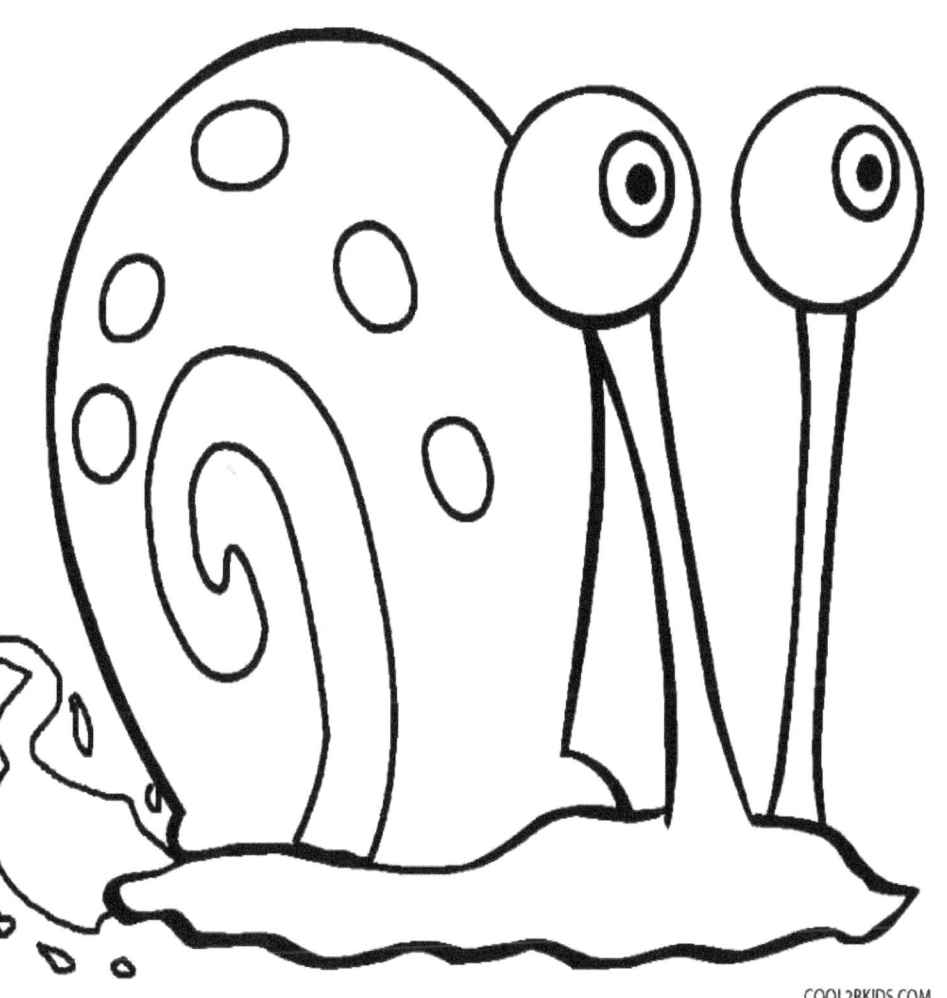

OTHERS

SOCCER

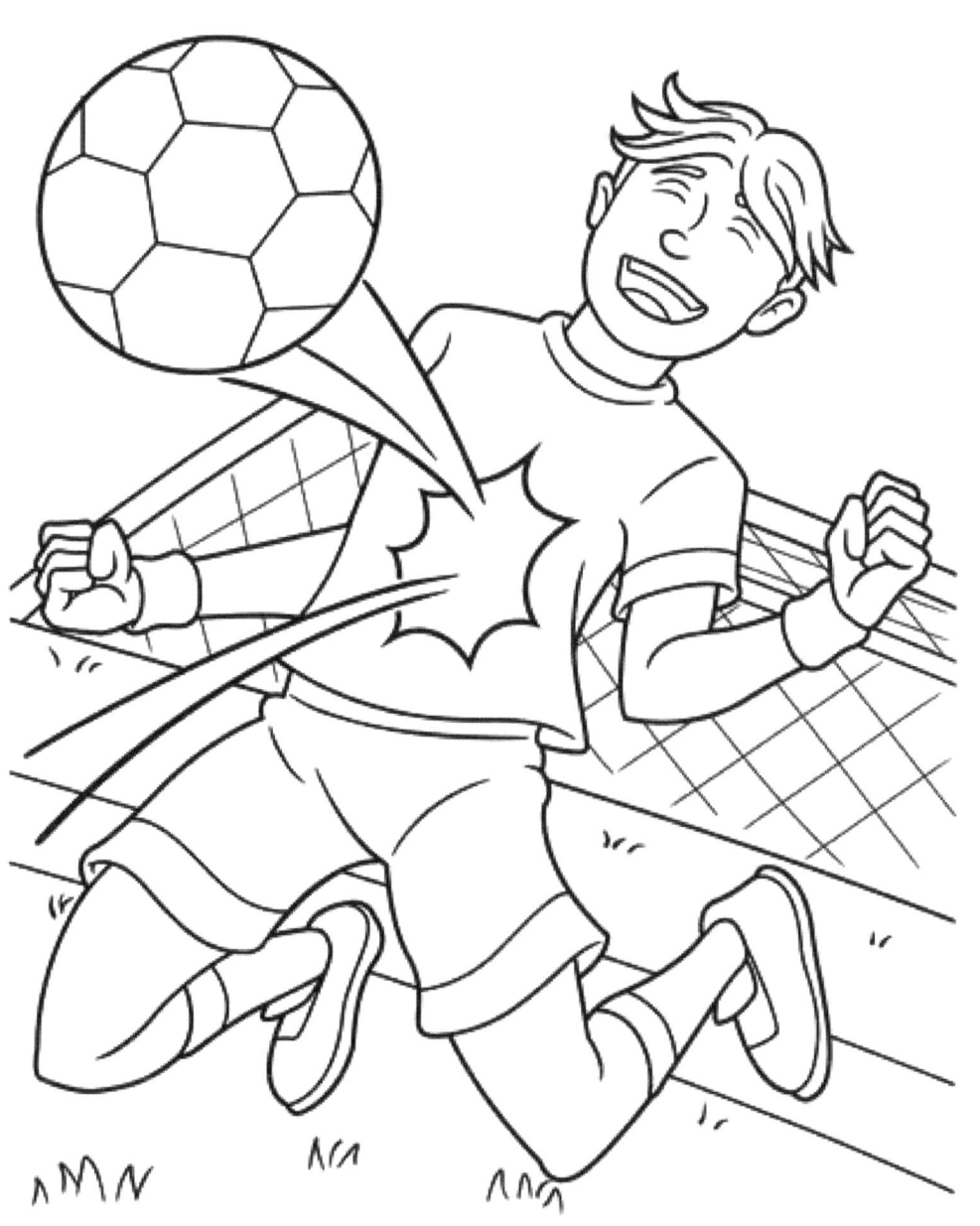

UNDER THE SEE

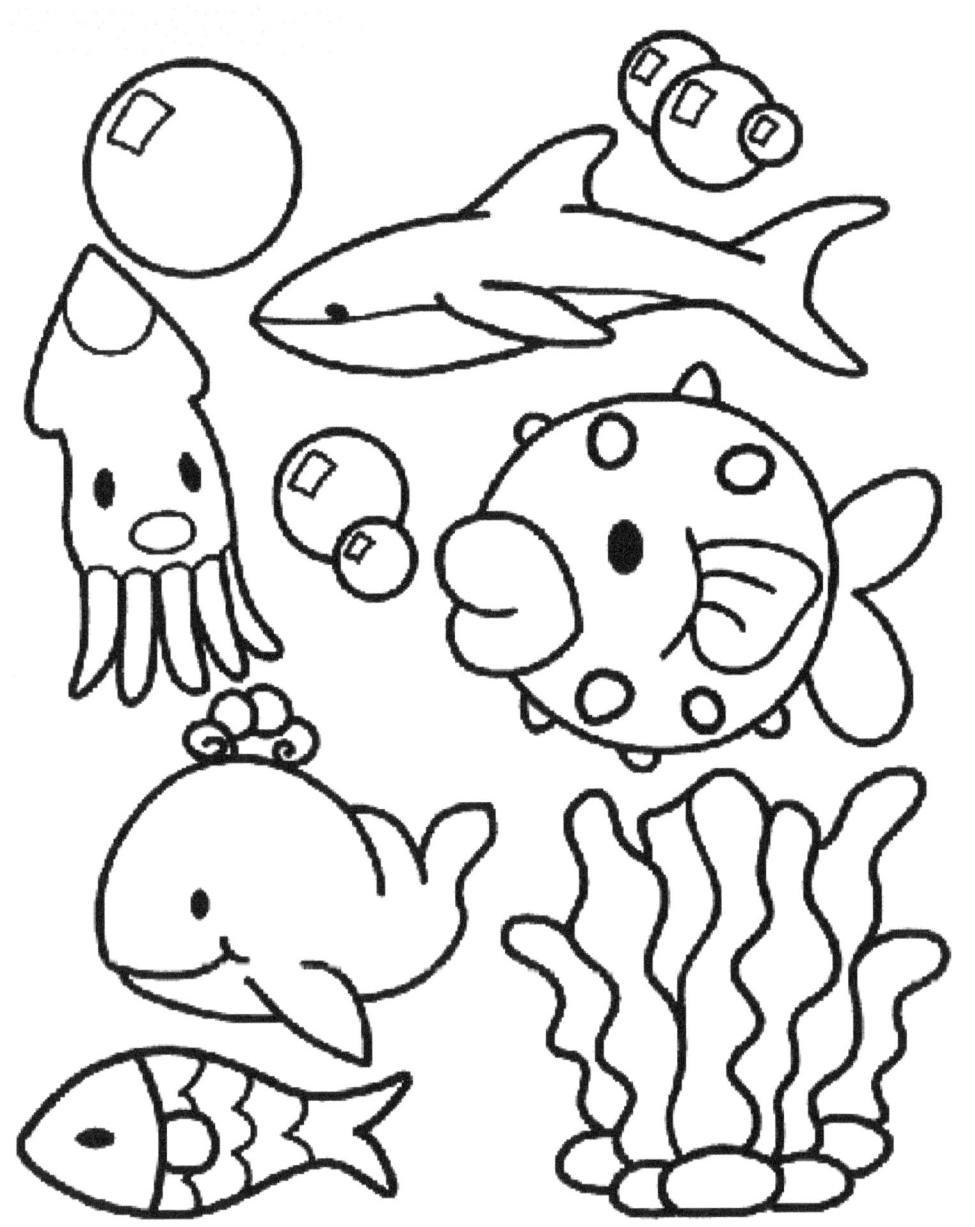

ST. PATRICS DAY

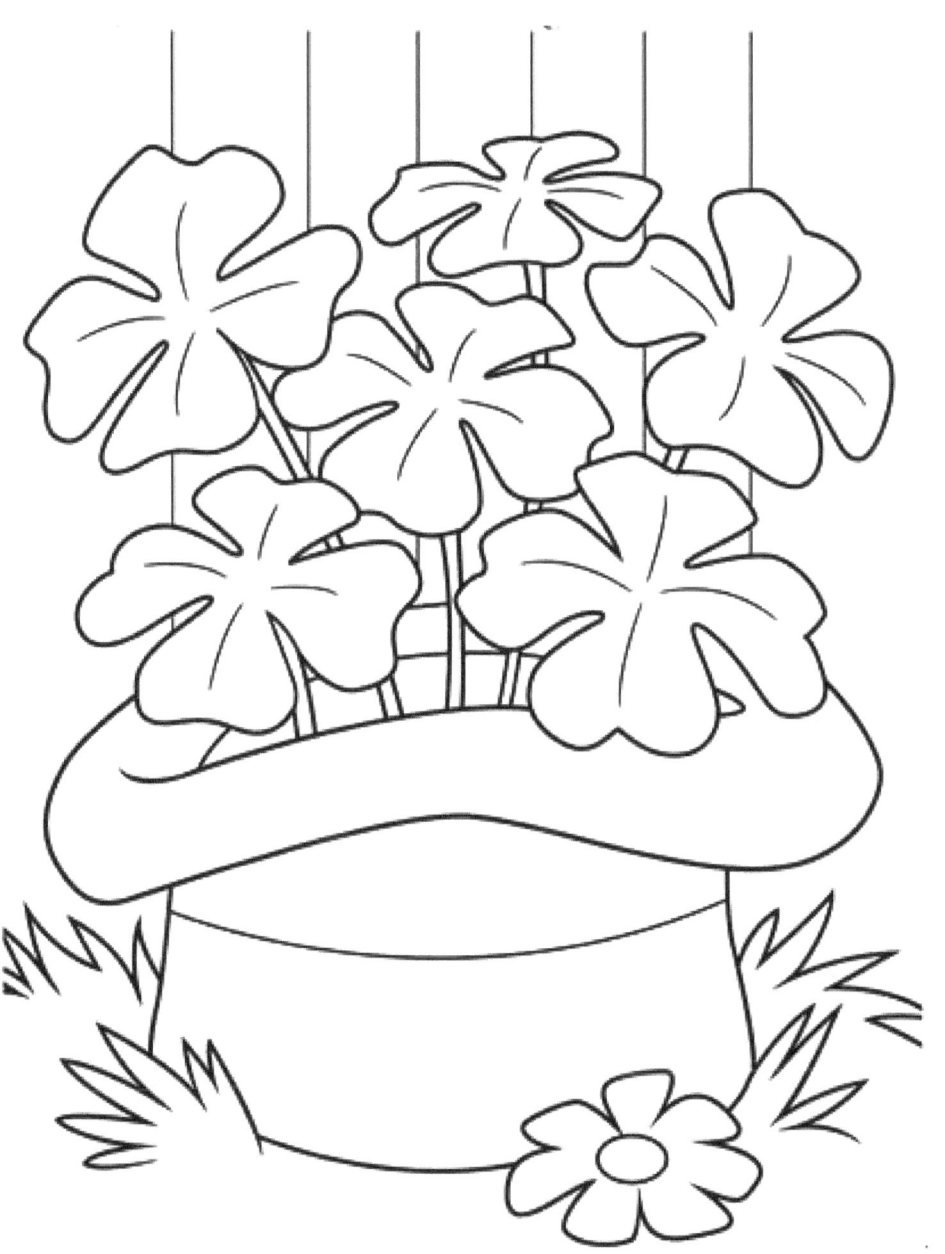

STAR WARS DARTH VADER

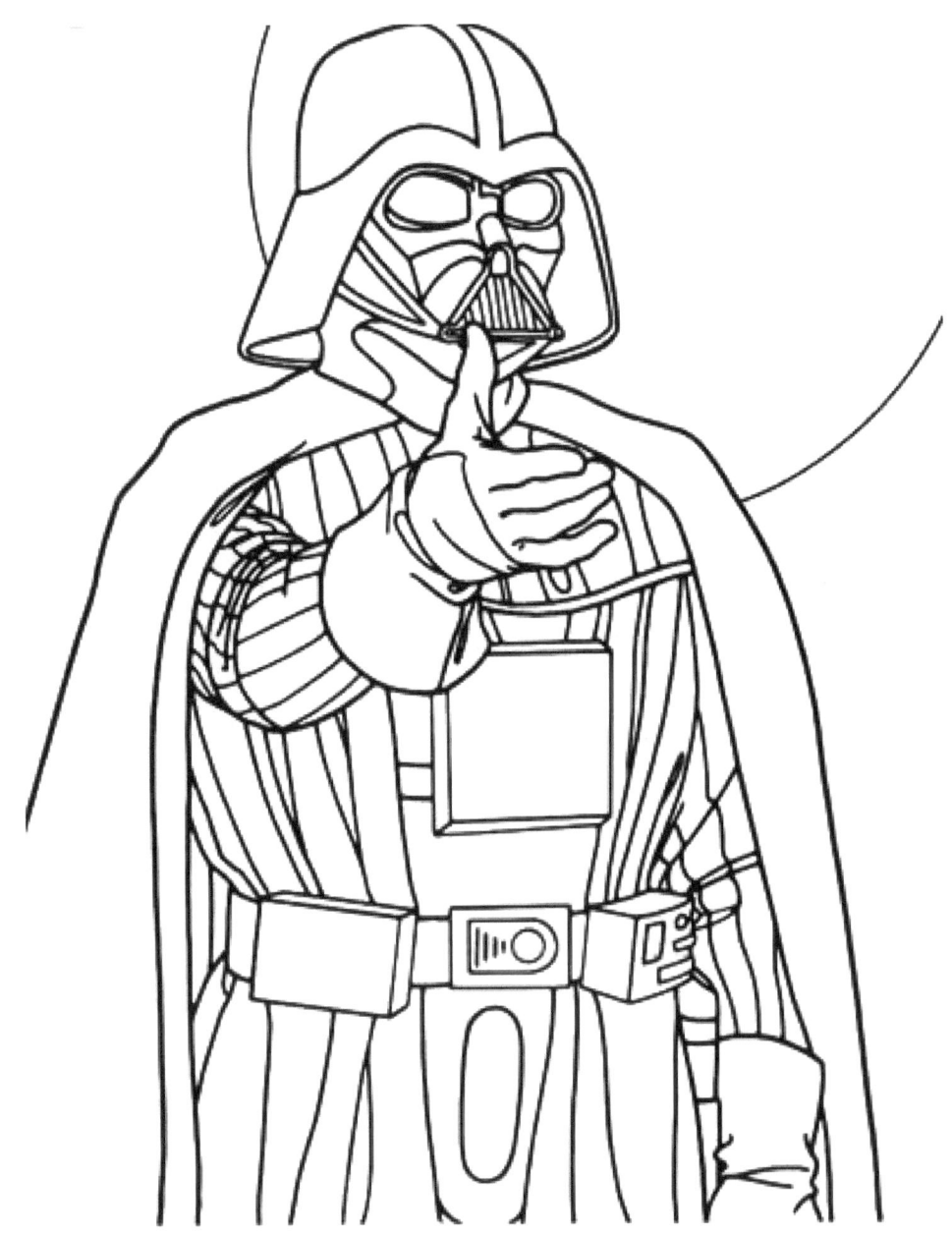

This is a coloring book made by deez prints ltd.

This ground breaking coloring book is all about building a kid's confidence, imagination, and spirit! The 22+ coloring pages encourage kids to think beyond social conventions and inspire conversations with adults.

Alla Bourbia 2020

www.ingramcontent.com/pod-product-compliance
Lightning Source LLC
Chambersburg PA
CBHW041945240526
45473CB00033B/612